Are there people from other countries?
pages 12-13

Can we swim in the Seine?
pages 14-15

there a pyramid at the Louvre?
pages 16-17

What does Champs-Élysées mean?
pages 22-23

Does Paris have any wild animals?
pages 24-25

Where are the big sports events held?
pages 32-33

Has Paris always existed?
pages 34-35

Does Paris hold any secrets?
pages 36-37

This publication was made by Milan Editions in collaboration with Karine Forest (French proofreader) and Corinna Anderson (English proofreader).

editionsmilan.com

ISBN: 978-2-7459-7768-7 – Legal deposit: 1st quarter 2016 – Printed in China

Paris

French text by **Stéphane Frattini**
English translation by **Charlotte Newman**
Illustrations by **Aurélie Grand**

MILAN

What are we going to visit today?

Paris, the capital of France, is the most visited city in the world. And yet, at just 11km wide, it isn't all that big. Its streets and districts however are filled with things to see and do!

The **Notre-Dame Cathedral** is the city's most popular monument: 40,000 people walk through its doors every day!

The **left bank** is half the size of the right bank. It is famous for its universities and artistic atmosphere. Small neighbourhoods in the south form quiet villages.

The city's wealthiest neighbourhoods are in the west part of the **right bank.** Boulevards and department stores fill the centre. To the east are the more working class districts.

Paris is divided into 20 **arrondissements** or **districts,** numbered in a spiral. Each one is governed by a mayor but the mayor of Paris is the big boss!

Why is the city round?

For a long time Paris was surrounded by city walls. The last of these were destroyed 100 years ago and replaced by a circular boulevard. This ring road now marks the city limits.

How many **metro** stations are there?

The metro has been growing ever since 1900. It now has just over 300 stations connected across 14 lines. In Paris you're never more than 500m from a station!

Getting trains across the **Seine** was a challenge. In 1904 workers built metal tunnel structures on the banks before pushing them right under the riverbed. Thousands of curious onlookers came to admire the feat.

Metro station **entrances** are usually easy to find. The oldest are in the **Art Nouveau** style. With their twists and turns they look like giant plants or insects.

Line 14 was the first line to use driverless **automatic** trains in 1998. They travel 39km/h on average, quite a lot faster than the standard trains at 21km/h. Board the train at the front for an impressive view!

Some metro lines cross over the Seine on viaducts. Others are **elevated** above ground along the centre of wide avenues.

What's the weather like in Paris?

The sky is often a luminous pale grey. It rains on average 160 days of the year but rarely a lot at once. Parisian winters are mild and its summers are rather hot and humid!

The city's **air quality** is closely monitored. If pollution levels get too high, measures are taken to reduce the number of cars and their speed.

The colour and style of the **street signs** have not changed since 1847. **Morris columns** are used to display posters for shows. As soon as the sun comes out, people flock to the many café **terraces.**

Facades on the old buildings are coated in light grey **plaster.** Fancier ones are covered in a beautiful cream-grey **limestone** that turns golden in the sunlight.

Why are the rooftops blue-grey?

Most of the rooftops are covered in zinc, a malleable metal that is easy to use. Some prestigious buildings, like the Opera, are covered in copper that turns green over time!

Are there people from other countries?

Like all large capital cities, Paris is a place where people from all over the world mingle and mix together. Out of the 2.25 million inhabitants, nearly two-thirds were born somewhere else!

The first train stations built in the 1840s lured many **country dwellers** to the city. One famous community was the "bougnats". They were people from the Auvergne region who ran cafés and sold coal.

This building houses **UNESCO**, the United Nations Organisation for Education, science and culture. A lot of foreigners work there and in the city's many embassies and international companies.

Some parts of the city have large **immigrant** populations. For example, a lot of Indians live near the Gare du Nord. Every year they celebrate the god Ganesha in a joyful procession.

On average, Paris welcomes 12 million foreign **tourists** a year. Americans are the largest group, followed by Chinese, Russian, and Middle Eastern tourists.

Can we swim in the Seine?

The river flows through Paris for 13 km. Its colour changes with the seasons from brown in the winter to green in the summer.

Along the riverbanks **booksellers** sell second-hand books and postcards. You might also see people fishing. The Seine is home to over 40 species of fish.

You can take a cruise on one of the **bateau-mouche tour boats** or hop on or off a **boat bus.** A lot of barges transport materials and goods to Paris's river port.

Paris has 37 bridges including 4 footbridges for pedestrians. The **Pont-Neuf** (meaning "new bridge") is actually now the city's oldest bridge. Built in 1607, it has withstood all of the Seine's floods!

Every summer tonnes of fine sand are trucked in for **Paris Plage**. The beach is a wonderful spot for all to enjoy. It would be best to use one of the floating pools installed on the river to have a swim.

Why is there a pyramid at the Louvre?

For seven centuries the Louvre palace was home to the kings of France. It is now the most visited museum in the world. The entrance is under the famous pyramid.

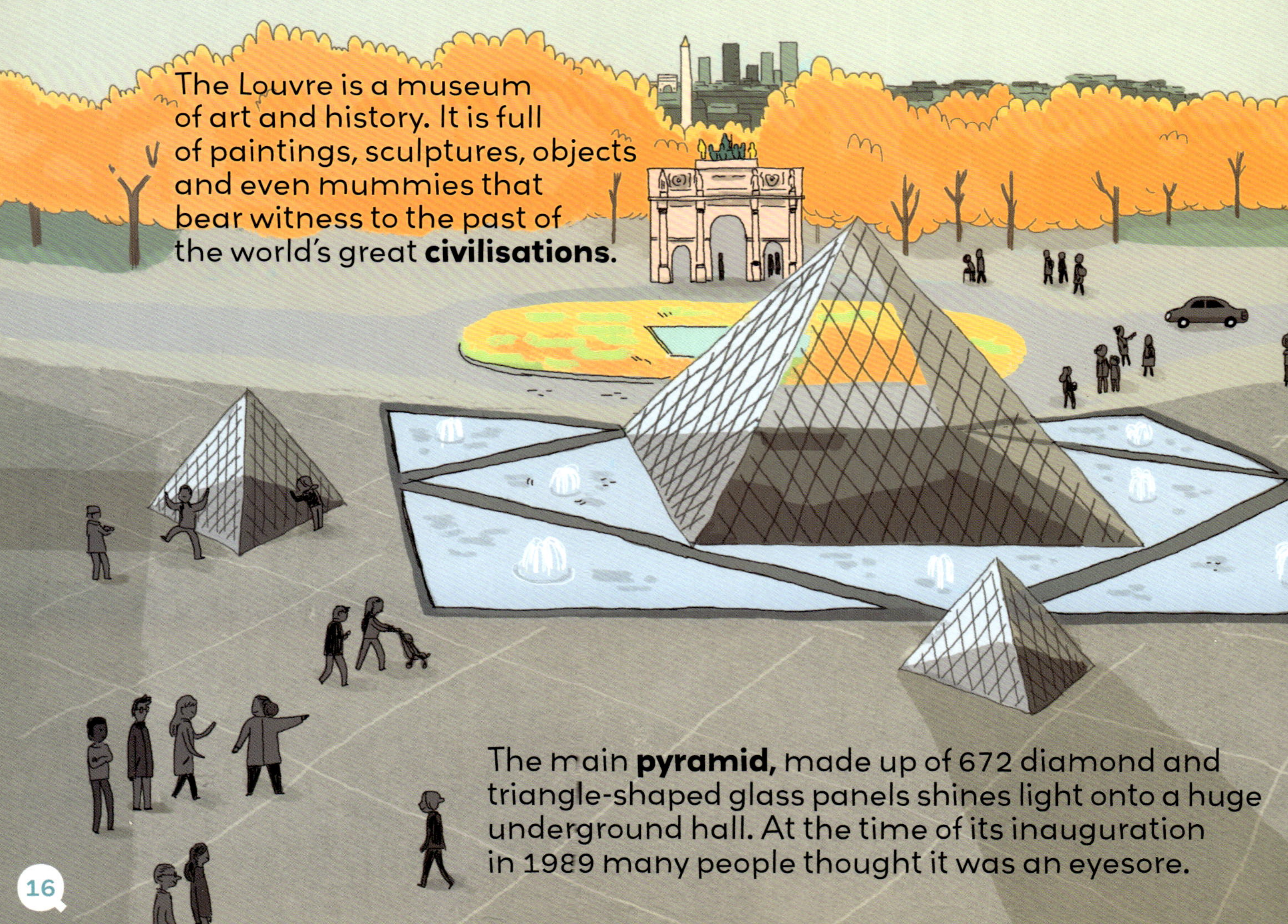

The Louvre is a museum of art and history. It is full of paintings, sculptures, objects and even mummies that bear witness to the past of the world's great **civilisations**.

The main **pyramid**, made up of 672 diamond and triangle-shaped glass panels shines light onto a huge underground hall. At the time of its inauguration in 1989 many people thought it was an eyesore.

The Louvre courtyard marks the beginning of the **Historical Axis of Paris**, an 8km line running straight through the Champs-Elysées all the way to the Grande Arche de la Défense.

How many works of art can we see?

The museum exibits 38,000 items, the most famous of which are Leonardo da Vinci's *Mona Lisa* and the *Venus de Milo*, an antique Greek sculpture. The archives hold 10 times more than what is on exhibit!

Can we climb to the top of the Eiffel Tower?

Erected in 1889 by the engineer Gustave Eiffel, the "300 meter tower" was built as a temporary attraction. Nobody has since dared to dismantle what has become a symbol of Paris!

It was made for a **Universal Exhibition (World's Fair)** using a new technique in metal construction. It took two years and 18,000 parts connected by 2.5 million bolts to build.

A glass floor panel was installed on the 1st **floor** in 2015, 57m above the ground level. You can see the ground below and all the tower's "iron lace" details. Are you brave enough to walk on it?

The tower was the world's tallest building until 1930. It now has an **antenna** making it 324m high, but visitors can only go as far as the 3rd floor at 276m.

To stop the tower from rusting, painters using mountain-climbing techniques give it a fresh **coat of paint** every seven years. It has three shades of bronze, from darkest at the bottom to lightest at the top.

Where does the President of France live?

All of France's important decisions are made in Paris, its capital city. Let's go and see the "Palace of the Republic" where the country's ministers, senators and deputies work.

The President lives in the **Elysée Palace.** This busy residence employs nearly 900 people, from the kitchens to 'Jupiter', its top-secret military control centre!

The 557 deputies of the **Assemblée Nationale** gather in the Bourbon Palace. They are elected by the people to monitor the government and participate in the Senate to vote on laws.

France's regional and municipal leaders elect the country's 348 senators. Their offices are in the **Luxembourg Palace**, which has a large public garden much loved by Parisians.

Paris is both a city and an administrative "department" of France (like a county). Its official department number is 75. The mayor of Paris presides over the City Council, which is housed in the **Hôtel de Ville (City Hall)**.

What does Champs-Élysées mean?

In Greek mythology the Elysian Fields are the paradise where heroes go to rest. Yet this wide avenue buzzes with its daily 300,000 visitors!

During King Louis XIV's reign it was a simple tree-lined lane that faced the **setting sun**. After the metro was installed in 1900 the avenue became a fashionable place for people to stroll.

Many protests, parades and other **major events** - even the finish of the Tour de France - are held on the Champs-Elysées. On 31 December, one million people gather there to celebrate the New Year.

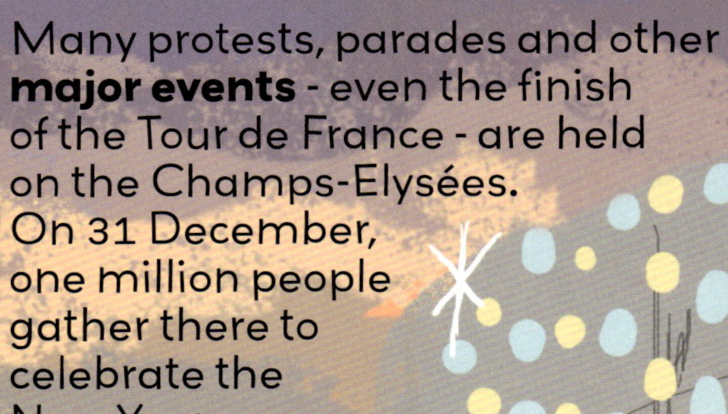

A large-scale **renovation** project is in the pipeline to make more pavement space and offer visitors more activities. The avenue will continue to surprise and delight!

Why is there a flame under the Arc de Triomphe?

The monument was inaugurated in 1836 and since 1920 it has watched over the tomb of an unknown soldier killed during the First World War. The flame is refuelled every night at 6:30 and never goes out!

Does Paris have any wild animals?

Paris is not very big and has fewer gardens than other capitals. And yet it has over 1,400 animal species!

Some buildings have **green roofs**, a paradise for insects and birds. Paris also has over 300 hives whose bees gather pollen from the city's park and balcony flowers.

Paris's public parks favour ecological gardening. Some have mini **wetlands** that are home to fragile species such as dragonflies and frogs.

Depending on the season, you can see up to 160 bird species in the city. The star is the **common kestrel**, a type of falcon. Around 50 couples nest in Paris, on the Notre-Dame Cathedral, the Arc de Triomphe and even the Eiffel Tower.

The **Petite Ceinture** or **small belt** is a partly abandoned former railway. It has become a nature reserve for wild animals, such as the red fox.

Why do lovers like Paris?

Paris has a reputation of being a romantic city. There is a real or imaginary love story for every corner and some are sure to have left a faint perfume in the air.

The city is a beautiful setting. You often see people in love **kissing** on a bench. Couples come to Paris from all over the world to share a special moment together!

A square in the Place des Abbesses at Montmartre has an "**I Love You**" **wall.** The wall is made up of 612 enamelled lava tiles covered in those magical words written in 250 languages.

Paris's **covered passages**, on the right bank, are the perfect place to stroll arm and arm. Filled with remarkable shops and cafés to sit and dream, these intimate passages weave in and out of streets around the Grands Boulevards.

Until 2015, lovers went to the **Pont des Arts** to attach a padlock to its railings before throwing the key into the Seine. The practice is now banned but the bridge is still an ideal spot for a dreamy kiss.

When are Paris's best festivals?

Paris hosts shows and festivals all year round, but a few big events make the whole city come to life. The atmosphere is electric!

On 14 July, France's **National Day** (also known as "**Bastille Day**"), the army parades down the Champs-Elysées. In the evening a fireworks display is set off at the Eiffel Tower. Firefighters organise balls for people to come and dance in their fire stations!

The first day of summer, 21 June, is also the **Fête de la Musique** or **Make Music Day.** Huge free concerts are held and amateurs come out to play music all over the city. The festival was invented in France in 1982 and is now celebrated in 120 countries!

The **Nuit Blanche** is an all-night event held one Saturday in October. Museums open their doors from dusk to dawn, and the city is filled with light displays. It's like walking in a dream!

The **Paris Carnival** disappeared in 1950 but has been rekindled in recent years for mardi gras in late February. A Caribbean-inspired **Tropical Carnival** is also held in June.

Are there a lot of artists in Paris?

Let's climb up the Montmartre Hill to the realm of street painters. Along with Montmartre this is one of the districts where modern art was invented. Today, there are a thousand ways to experience art in Paris!

Around the 1880s, **impressionists** revolutionised the art world. They began painting outside and stopped trying to convey reality but rather wanted to portray an impression. You can admire their masterpieces in the Musée d'Orsay.

Montmartre saw the birth of the first **artists' estates** where each artist could rent a workshop. Picasso, Modigliani, Miró – most of the great artists of the 20th Century lived here!

The French State and the City of Paris also have a **cultural** policy to support the arts. Many artists are invited as residents to create world-renowned projects that everyone can enjoy.

Why can we see people painting in museums?

Some artists are authorised to come and copy a painting. The size must be different from the original and they need to finish in three months.
It's fascinating to watch them repeat the gestures of the great painters.

Where are the big sports events held?

Sports and Paris have a long history together. This is where fencing and cycling began for example. The city still hosts major competitions watched all over the globe.

The **Stade de France** is located to the north in neighbouring suburb Saint-Denis. The stadium opened in 1998 for the football world cup, which France won that year. The whole country went crazy!

The French Open is held late May to early June at the **Rolland-Garros** tennis stadium. It's the only one of the four Grand Slam tournaments to be played on a clay court, making for an exciting game.

The **Paris Marathon** is one of the world's biggest, second only to New York. The race is held on the right bank starting at the Champs-Elysées and passing two loops through Bois de Boulogne and Bois de Vincennes.

The **Palais de Bercy**, known for its sloping lawns, can hold up to 20,000 spectators. Using a system of sliding spaces it can host all types of sports, even on water or ice!

Has Paris always existed?

Here we are around the year 200 at the time of Roman Gaul. The small city of Lutetia has settled on the left bank of the Seine. It has barely more than 10,000 inhabitants but attracts a lot of visitors!

Paved straight streets and spacious houses surround the public gathering area, the **forum.** Aqueducts bring water to the public baths. The city is more comfortable than it would be for centuries to come!

Before the Roman conquest, Île de la Cité was the only area occupied by the Gaul tribe **Parisii** with their thatched cottages. The right bank was marshland.

The **arenas** could seat up to 15,000 spectators and people came from afar to see the show. Like the rest of the town, they were destroyed in Barbarian raids after year 450.

Since when has the city been called Paris?

The settlement's first name was Lutetia in Latin, undoubtedly derived from the Celtic word luta meaning marsh. Around the year 300, the city was renamed Paris, an abbreviation of the Latin Civitas Parisiorum, "the city of the Parisii".

Does Paris hold any secrets?

Paris has existed for 20 centuries! It is sure to whisper a few mysteries from times past into the ear of anyone curious enough to listen.

The oldest monument in the capital dates back to 1300 years B.C. This is the **Luxor obelisk**, a present from Egypt that was relocated to the Place de la Concorde in 1836.

The left bank has 300km of abandoned quarries. Some sections, called the **Catacombs**, hold the bones of six million Parisians transferred from early cemeteries and can be visited. That's a spooky tour!

In Square Viviani, near Notre-Dame, grows Paris's **oldest tree.** This black locust was brought back from America in 1601 by King Henry IV's botanist. Just think of all the tales it could tell...

At 51 rue de Montmorency sits Paris's oldest house built in 1407 by **Nicolas Flamel.** This alchemist is said to have found the secret of the Philosopher's Stone that could turn lead into gold!

Other books in this series include

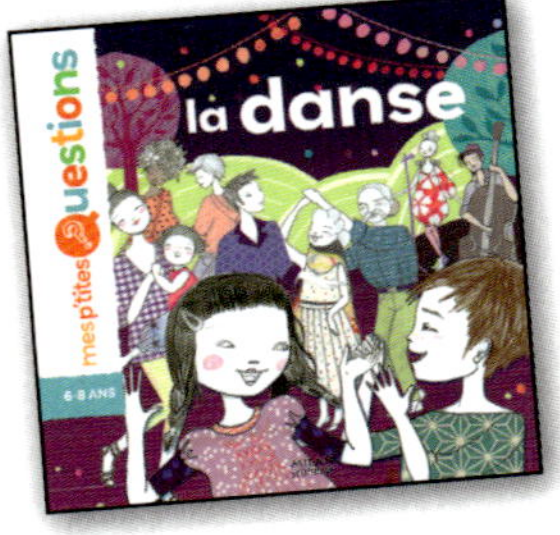

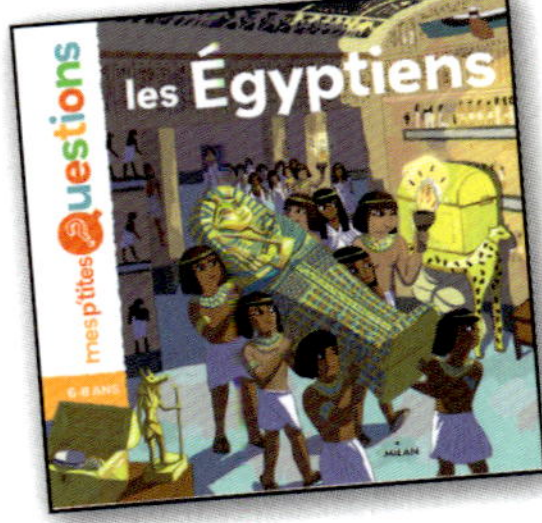

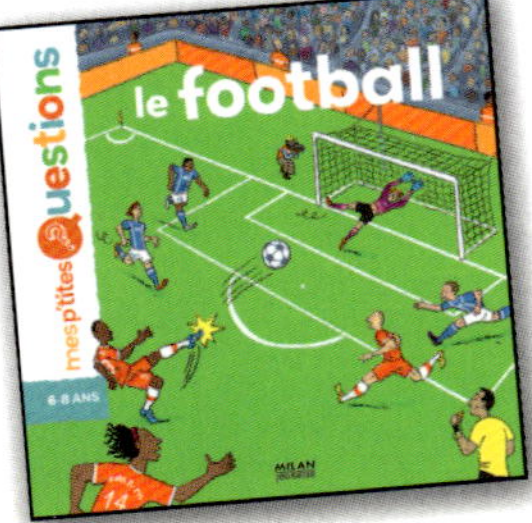